THE ULTIMATE P(
TRAVEL GUIDE(2023)

What to know before you visit, Best Things to do, Must Visit Places and Attractions (Essential Travel Budget, Safety, and Tips)

Patrick Wyles

CONTENTS

INTRODUCTION 7

CHAPTER ONE...9

    THE BEST ATTRACTIONS -WHAT SHOULD YOU SEE IN PORTUGAL? 9

CHAPTER TWO 33

    BEST THINGS TO DO IN PORTUGAL...33
    THE BEST TIME TO VISIT PORTUGAL 40
    HOW TO GET AROUND IN PORTUGAL 41

CHAPTER THREE 49

    15 ESSENTIAL DISHES TO TRY IN PORTUGAL.............................49

CHAPTER FOUR..67

    WHERE TO STAY IN PORTUGAL: BEST PLACES & HOTELS 67

CHAPTER FIVE 81

    10 BEST BEACH RESORTS IN PORTUGAL 81
    5 BEST DAY TRIPS IN PORTUGAL...89

CHAPTER SIX 103

    BEST THINGS TO DO WITH KIDS IN LISBON 103

CHAPTER SEVEN 113

    THINGS YOU NEED TO KNOW BEFORE GOING TO PORTUGAL...........113
    10 WAYS TO TRAVEL TO PORTUGAL ON A TIGHT BUDGET...............117
    14 Top Travel Tips For Portugal That'll Help You Plan A Better & A More Hassle-Free Trip 120

CHAPTER EIGHT 131

    CONCLUSION 131

INTRODUCTION

Portugal is one of Europe's top tourism destinations, located on the western coast of the Iberian Peninsula. It has a rich cultural and architectural legacy because to its long history as a proud naval nation. Portugal, being the birthplace of several historical civilizations, continues to astound visitors. See the spectacular Tower of Belem in Lisbon's capital, or go to Sao Jorge Fortress, a hilltop Moorish castle and palace remains. Porto's Baroque and Romanesque churches, symphony halls, and museums enchant visitors from the north. Some of the world's best wine is made in vineyards in the northern countryside.

The spectacular northern mountain ranges of Portugal's interior blend with the broad rolling plains of the country's sun-drenched middle regions. Some of Europe's best beaches are found in the south, where gorgeous coves and warm, shallow waters are surrounded by some of the best beaches in the world. Stone-built villages, charming towns, and cosmopolitan cities dot the landscape, offering historic palaces and castles, museums, and monasteries to visit.

Portugal preserves the rustic qualities that its European counterparts have lost. It is a land of delectable cuisine, fine ports, immaculate beaches, and medieval villages perched atop picturesque hills. The picturesque ports along the Tajo and the towering cliffs of the Serra de Estrela, combined with the Moorish neighborhoods and high rises of Lisbon, provide for a truly magical travel experience.

The stunning beachfront cliffs near Lagos can be seen along Portugal's southern Atlantic coast. With so much to see and do all around the nation, a trip to Portugal will leave you with lifelong memories.

CHAPTER ONE

The Best Attractions -What should you see in Portugal?

Portugal's topography is capped by castles and stunning walled towns, making it one of Europe's oldest extant countries. Then there are the mountains and the lovely long beaches, as well as the hearty homecooked food and world-class wine, you'll be surprised at how affordable it is when you visit Portugal.

Travel Facts about Portugal

- Portuguese is a language with 10 distinct dialects.
- The Euro (€) is the official currency of the European Union.
- Geographically, Portugal has 1793 kilometers of coastline, which includes the perimeter of its islands. Spain is its only neighbor.
- Ten million people live in Portugal, with ten times as many living in other countries, the majority of whom are in Brazil.
- Exports - Portugal is the seventh largest wine producer in the world and supplies half of the world's cork.
- History and heritage abound in Portugal, with cities like Évora and Guimares among the twelve UNESCO World Heritage Sites.

Mosteiro dos Jerónimos

Belém is associated with Portugal's Golden Age of Exploration. In the 15th and 16th centuries, brave navigators set sail from the shoreline of this Lisbon suburb on lengthy and risky expeditions to navigate unknown oceans and map new lands.

In 1498, one of these mariners, Vasco da Gama, discovered the maritime path to India, and King Manuel I commissioned a monument to commemorate his feat, which has become a permanent emblem of the country's remarkable era of conquest and growth. The Mosteiro dos Jerónimos is now one of the country's most cherished and revered structures, and it is a must-see for all visitors.

The church and monastery encapsulate the spirit of the era and have some of the best examples of Manueline architecture in Portugal; the South Portal's ornate decoration is stunning.

The lovely cloister on the inside is similarly extravagant. The tombs of Vasco da Gama and other national figures, like Lus de

Cames, Portugal's finest poet and historian of the discoveries, are appropriately housed in the chapel.

Oceanário de Lisboa, Lisbon

Lisbon's oceanarium, which is arguably Portugal's most popular and family-friendly visitor attraction, was wonderfully designed to highlight the world's different ocean environments. This oceanarium is one of Europe's greatest and largest, with a diverse collection of fish and aquatic species.

The ecosystems of the Atlantic, Pacific, Indian, and Antarctic oceans are recreated in four different seascapes. A massive center tank, visible from several levels, is teeming with sharks, rays, and other finned wonders and deep-sea creatures. Smaller tropical species kept in individual aquaria arranged around the main tank appear to be swimming alongside their larger cousins because to the clear plexiglass construction.

The open-air settings, where penguins, sea otters, and other charming and cuddly birds and creatures co-exist in blissful harmony, complement this wonderful display.

Palácio Nacional de Sintra, Lisbon Coast

Sintra's magnificent position, nestled in the midst of a wooded mountain range, is incentive enough to pay this lovely, verdant town a visit. Because of the beauty and importance of the collection of historic visitor attractions located in and around Sintra Velha, UNESCO has designated the location as a World Heritage cultural landscape.

Sintra oozes romanticism and was a popular summer resort for the Portuguese kings and queens, as well as an enticing destination for many artists and poets, including Lord Byron and William Beckford. The old town is a maze of cobblestone streets lined with charming town houses painted in pastel pink, mustard, and lilac hues. The lovely Palácio Nacional de

Sintra dominates the central square, which is surrounded by little streets.

Sintra's National Palace, easily identified by its massive conical chimneys, originates from the late 14th century and is Portugal's oldest surviving palace. The building is lavishly equipped and is divided into multiple storeys, each with its own theme and décor. The majestic Sala dos Brases, a sparkling domed chamber adorned with the coats of arms of 72 noble Portuguese families, is a highlight.

Kayaking the Lisbon Coast

A wonderful maritime activity is paddling out into the sea to explore the Lisbon coast by kayak. Paddling the coast provides a fantastic excuse to exercise in a salt-laced, pristine setting, in addition to adding another layer to the sightseeing experience.

Indeed, Lisbon's proximity to the sea allows for a variety of interesting water sports, and exploring the beaches, bays, and coves that run between the Portuguese city and the resort town of Cascais is a wonderful way to spend a day.

Beyond the area, the crystal-clear waters off the Serra da Arrábida Natural Park, which includes Setubal and Sesimbra, provide a one-of-a-kind scene of majestic, old sea cliffs teeming with birds.

The majority of the coastline here is protected by a marine reserve, which includes the stunningly beautiful Ribeira do Cavalo beach.

Torre de Belém, Lisbon

The Torre de Belém, a Lisbon icon and one of Portugal's most popular historic structures, is a symbol of the Age of Discovery and the exploration voyages of the 15th and 16th centuries.

The tower, which was completed in 1521 as a stronghold to guard the approaches to the river Tagus, is considered a military architectural masterpiece. The façade is a confection of elegantly carved stone, defined by maritime symbols such as twisted rope and the armillary sphere, and was designed in the Manueline style by Francisco de Arruda. The ornamentation is enhanced by an exquisite Renaissance loggia. UNESCO has designated the tower as a World Heritage Site because of its cultural significance.

Convento do Cristo, Tomar

Convento do Cristo, Tomar

The Convento do Cristo, one of Portugal's most important historic sites, is protected by a huge castle that towers over the picturesque riverside village of Tomar.

The Convent of Christ, founded in 1160 as the headquarters of the Knights Templar, is as awe-inspiring as it is mysterious, its masonic past vivid and enchanting. The medieval Charola, the original Templar church, lies at its heart, beautifully ornamented and replete with all the bizarre symbolism connected with the Order of Christ.

The Manueline flourishes of the 16th-century cloisters enchant tourists, and their hidden spiral stairs taunt them. The convent's exquisite Manueline window, created by master sculptor Diogo de Arruda, is one of Portugal's most architecturally appealing features.

Bom Jesus do Monte, Braga

Bom Jesus do Monte, Portugal's finest religious sanctuary, is located six kilometers east of Braga on a wooded slope and is one of the country's most prominent pilgrimage sites.

This magnificent complex includes a gigantic Baroque Escadaria (stairway) and the church of Bom Jesus, as well as multiple chapels with sculptured scenes from the Passion of Christ, fountains at various points along the long ascent, and statues of biblical, mythological, and symbolic figures.

Climbing the bottom half of the 116-meter decorative granite stairway leads to a steep Sacred Way with chapels depicting the 14 Stations of the Cross.

The white, interlaced Escadório dos Cinco Sentidos, located in the middle, portrays the five senses through artistically carved statues.

The Staircase of the Three Virtues, which leads to the church, is the final piece. It represents Faith, Hope, and Charity. Your efforts will be rewarded with a breathtaking view of the surrounding landscape. A classic 1882 funicular whisks guests to the top in about three minutes for the less active.

Hiking the Gerês Mountain Range

The Serra do Gerês is a breathtakingly beautiful mountain range in northern Portugal's secluded Minho area. The granite peaks that characterize the nature of this enormous national park, set within the gorgeous Parque Nacional da Peneda-Gerês, one of the top locations to visit in Portugal, are among the highest and most spectacular in the country.

The Gerês Mountains, one of Portugal's most popular natural attractions, attract walkers, hikers, and outdoor enthusiasts to one of Europe's last great wildernesses, a stark and rugged landscape known for its lush valleys dotted with shimmering lakes, a scattering of traditional villages, rare flora and fauna, and a way of life that has all but disappeared from the country's mountain regions.

The area is crisscrossed by ancient granite trails, which are signposted for hikers to follow, either as a short stroll or a challenging day trek. Most of the tracks are 10 to 16 kilometers in length and of varying grades.

Universidade de Coimbra

King Dinis created the Universidade de Coimbra in 1290, making it Portugal's oldest educational institution. The historic buildings of the Velha Universidade, or old Coimbra University, surround a lovely colonnaded center square, the Paço das Escolas, which has been designated as a UNESCO World Heritage Site.

The university's Alta and Sofia wings - a former royal home – have a variety of notable features, including the magnificent Biblioteca Joanina, a lavishly decorated library built in 1717 by King Joo V.

The journey also includes a visit to the opulent 16th-century Capela de S. Miguel. Climbers with a fear of heights can ascend the iconic 18th-century clock tower for a spectacular view over Coimbra, one of the country's most beautiful cities.

Museu Calouste Gulbenkian, Lisbon

Lisbon is home to some truly world-class museums, including the Museu Calouste Gulbenkian, which is one of the best. Calouste Sarkis Gulbenkian, a wealthy Armenian oil entrepreneur who bequeathed his precious trove to the Portuguese nation upon his death in 1955, left the museum with 6,000 items, all of which belonged to one man: Calouste Sarkis Gulbenkian.

Simply put, this is one of Europe's best art collections. The displays span over 4,000 years, from classical and oriental antiquity to early twentieth-century European art. No other museum has such a diverse collection of art from around the world, and visitors can spend hours poring over treasures like the 11 Roman medallions discovered in Egypt; 16th-century illustrated manuscripts; Rubens, Rembrandt, and Turner masterpieces; Louis XV and Louis XVI furniture; and Rene Lalique Art Nouveau jewelry.

The museum is surrounded by lovely grounds that are ideal for picnics, especially in the summer.

Castelo de Guimarães

Guimares was formerly the capital of the kingdom of Portucale, and it was here that Portugal's first ruler, Dom Afonso Henriques, was born in 1110.

The Castelo de Guimares, designated as a World Heritage Site by UNESCO for its collection of ancient monuments arranged in and around the old town center, best reflects the town's role in defining the nation's culture and heritage - it even appears on the Portuguese coat of arms.

The stronghold, erected on an elevated outcrop of granite in the 10th century but significantly expanded by Henry of Burgundy two centuries later, consists of a central keep – the Torre de Menagem – encircled by large battlements and defended towers.

Dom Afonso was christened at the little Romanesque church of So Miguel, which is located just outside the castle walls, and tourists can see the font inside. A walk along the ramparts is magnificent, but climbing the keep provides the best views.

Torre de Clérigos, Oporto

One of Oporto's most recognizable monuments is the spindly, needle-like Torre de Clérigos. This slender tower, standing 75 meters above the streets and overlooking the old town, was erected by Nicolau Nasoni in the 18th century and emits a powerful sense of the Baroque. The tower, which was built as part of the Igreja dos Clérigos, was completed in 1763 and was the tallest building in Oporto at the time.

Visitors must climb upwards of 200 stairs to reach the top, but the exertion will be forgotten as you take in the genuinely wonderful views of the city and the river Douro.

Castelo de São Jorge, Lisbon

Castelo de S. Jorge is the city's most visible historic monument, with its commanding position atop a hill overlooking Lisbon's lively Baixa (downtown) sector. The foundations of this beautiful castle, which is popular with both locals and tourists, date from the late 12th century, when King Afonso Henriques recovered the city from the Moors and erected a palace over the ruins of their hilltop fortification.

The royal house was expanded and strengthened with substantial battlements in 1511. Much of the structure was destroyed in the great earthquake of 1755, and what is left now is largely the result of extensive reconstruction.

It's a lot of fun to explore the castle. The ramparts and castellated towers, one of which, Torre de Ulisses, includes a camera obscura that projected views of the city onto the internal walls, are open to visitors. The walls surround an archaeological site that includes the remnants of the original Alcáçova palace as well as early Moorish foundations.

The most beautiful views of Lisbon and the river may be found on the observation terrace at the entrance.

Sé (cathedral) and Roman Temple, Évora

Roman Temple with the Evora Cathedral in the distance

Évora, one of Portugal's most lovely cities, is located in the sun-drenched Alentejo province in southern Portugal. The town began to take shape under Moorish administration, with its network of small roads and alleyways typical of Islamic urban planning. The Romans established themselves here around 57 BC, but it was under Moorish rule that the town began to take shape. The Sé, Évora's majestic cathedral and one of several

19

stunning visitor attractions in the ancient town, was built after the Christian reconquest.

After enjoying the interior of this historic religious edifice, tourists can go up to the roof, which offers great views of the surrounding area, which was consecrated in 1204.

The Roman Temple, Évora's most famous structure, is close by. This is the most spectacular Roman structure in the country, dating from the 2nd or 3rd century AD. Évora's historic legacy is so significant that UNESCO has designated it as a World Heritage Site.

Alentejo by Horseback

Exploring the Alentejo on horseback is one of the best things to do, whether you're following a narrow, babbling stream, traversing a flower-flecked meadow, or slogging over a soft, sandy pathway.

The region is recognized for its love of horses, particularly the elegant and mild-mannered Lusitano breed, which is synonymous with places like Alter do Cho, which is home to the Coudelaria de Alter stud.

Rides in the countryside or along the shore can be experienced with expert guides who were almost born in the saddle. Comporta is a popular seaside resort; inland, visit Alcácer do Sal on the Sado River and Ourique, which is deep in the forested interior.

Mosteiro Pálacio Nacional de Mafra

The magnificent Mafra National Palace and Monastery rises over the lovely agricultural village of Mafra and is a stunning display of opulence.

The construction of what was supposed to be a small monastery and basilica, commissioned by Dom Joo V to commemorate the birth of the king's first child, began in 1717.

However, as the royal coffers grew larger as a result of the income from Brazil, the project took on a new level, and a massive Baroque palace was eventually erected, richly furnished with exotic furnishings and various works of art.

The monastery, palace, cathedral, and basilica can all be visited as part of a tour. The exquisite marble-floored library, where more than 40,000 rare and valuable books line Rococo-style wooden bookcases – one of Europe's most important collections of manuscripts and literature – is without a doubt one of the National Palace and Monastery of Mafra's indisputable highlights.

Igreja de Santo António and the Museu Municipal, Lagos

The Municipal Museum in Lagos houses the Algarve's most unusual collection of archeology and anthropology. The marvelously eclectic display of local handicrafts, curios, and antiquities, which includes objects like a cork altarpiece and a realistic constructed scale model of an imaginary Algarve village, brilliantly shows the region's diverse culture and heritage.

The spectacular Opus Vermiculatum Roman Mosaic, discovered in 1933 by the museum's creator, Dr José Formosinho, is a highlight. The Igreja de Santo António, with its stunning interior of exquisite gilt carvings and colorful azulejos panels, is the tour's final stop.

Silves Castle

Silves, formerly known as Xelb, was the capital of the Moorish Algarve, and the Arabs dubbed the region al-Gharb.

The village was known as a center of study in the early 12th century, a gathering place for Islamic writers, philosophers, and geographers. The Moors built a huge fortress on an elevated vantage point overlooking the town to defend the locals.

The citadel was later captured by Crusaders and exists today as a permanent symbol of Moorish dominance and Christian Reconquest. It is the Algarve's most spectacular historic site and one of Portugal's best castles. Its massive red sandstone cliffs provide an enticing ochre glow over the charming riverside town of Silves below.

Early August is the time to visit for the annual Medieval Festival held outside the fortified battlements.

Cross-Border Zipline, Alcoutim

This is one of the country's most adventurous and radical tourist attractions, spanning Spain and Portugal and currently the world's only cross-border zipline. The line, which runs from Sanlcar de Guadiana in Spain's Huelva province to

Alcoutim in the far north of the Algarve, is 720 meters long and spans the large and flowing River Guadiana.

Participants take off from a takeoff platform high above the river, overlooking the peaceful village of Sanlcar, wearing full safety belts and helmets. They practically fly through time as they cross the river at speeds of 70 to 80 kilometers per hour, gaining one hour due to the time difference between the two countries.

The ride is thrilling and completely unique, providing a completely unique Algarve visitor experience. It's not every day that you can boast of traveling from one country to another in under one minute!

Palácio da Bolsa, Oporto

The elegant Palácio da Bolsa, the city's historic stock exchange house, is one of Oporto's many appealing tourist attractions. The palace, which was built by businessmen in the mid-nineteenth century on the site of the former So Francisco monastery, is located inside the old city limits and is thus designated as a UNESCO World Heritage Site.

The opulent interior reflects the influx of money into the city at the period, and a walk of the magnificent halls and galleries reveals opulence and luxury on par with any royal palace. The spectacular Salo rabe, or Arabian Room, epitomizes this richness. The gorgeously gilded salon is enveloped with blue and gold Moorish-style ornamentation that shimmers like Aladdin's cave and is inspired by the Alhambra in Granada.

Côa Valley Archaeological Park (Parque Arqueológico do Vale do Côa), Vila Nova de Foz Côa

Thousands of rock engravings from prehistoric times engraved into enormous slabs of granite were discovered by a team of engineers surveying a valley of the River Côa in northeastern Portugal in the early 1990s while planning the construction of a dam. It was a once-in-a-lifetime opportunity. the dam project was finally abandoned, and the carvings — which depict horses, livestock, weapons, human and abstract figures and date back to 22,000 BCE – were classified as a UNESCO World Heritage Site.

Visitors can now join a guided trip in all-terrain vehicles to see this ancient rock art maintained in situ at the Côa Valley Archaeological Park. They may also learn more about the artwork's roots and explore the valley through multimedia, photography, and photographs of the engravings at the fantastic Côa Museum, which is located at the park's entrance.

Paiva Walkways (Passadiços do Paiva), Arouca

This award-winning amenity, known as the Paiva Walkways, checks all the green boxes. The Paiva Walkways, located outside of Arouca, central Portugal, a 70-kilometer drive north of Aveiro, provide a challenging but highly rewarding eight-kilometer hike over an elevated boardwalk that dips, climbs, and meanders through the Arouca Geopark – an unspoiled landscape of outstanding beauty and a biodiversity hotspot.

The hike begins at Areinho and follows the clean Paiva River downstream for part of the route. You'll soon be wandering through a harsh, rarely-visited landscape of tranquil, verdant woodland and deep, yawning gorges.

You'll encounter tumbling waterfalls and calm, mirror-like pools along the route. The walk frequently entails climbing long flights of zigzagging steps up steep inclines: the path truly puts stamina and physical fitness to the test.

It takes about 2.5 hours to finish the trek, which concludes in Espiunca. Sunscreen, energy foods, and lots of water should all be included in your travel kit.

CHAPTER TWO
Best things to do in Portugal
Adventure sports

Portugal is known for its beaches, golf courses, and tennis centers, but it also offers a great climate for adventure sports, with several places now offering paragliding, abseiling, rafting, canyoning, caving, mountain biking, and 4WD trips. The mountains, particularly the Serra da Estrela and Peneda-Gerês parks, and the major rivers (Douro, Mondego, and Zêzere), offer the most opportunities, but many of the smaller natural parks and reserves also have local adventure firms.

Swimming, surfing, and windsurfing are some of the most popular water sports.

When you visit Portugal, there's a good chance you'll take in some of the country's breathtaking coastline. The Algarve boasts the country's most popular sandy beaches, many of which are sheltered in bays, and the sea in the eastern Algarve is the warmest. The western coast has some spectacular beaches, but they are exposed to the full force of the Atlantic Ocean, making for excellent surfing and wind-surfing chances - Portugal travel at its best. The Algarve's more protected west coast is ideal for both novices and expert surfers; don't miss out on a trip to Portugal to try it out.

Hiking and walking are two popular activities.

While there is only one national park in Portugal, the Parque Nacional da Peneda-Gerês in the north, there are over forty more protected places that offer fantastic treks. The lesser-trodden trails of Portugal's highest mountains deserve special notice; taking in historic communities, waterfalls, windswept rocky plateaus, and breathtaking views, routes in the Parque Natural da Serra da Estrela are a must-see for ambitious hikers visiting the country. It's possible that you'll want to hire a trekking guide from Portugal.

The limestone caverns of the Serras do Aire e Candeeiros, the island retreat of the Ilha Berlenga (reachable from Peniche), and the lagoons, dunes, and marshes of the Ria Formosa are just a few of Portugal's other stunning trekking environments.

Traditional entertainment, culture, and history

You will not be short of historic sights to see in Portugal, regardless of which location you visit. From Alfama, Lisbon's historic core, with its Moorish castle, to Monsaraz, a sparsely populated medieval village. It rises high above a plain of vineyards and olive groves, with a beautiful castle and quaint lanes dotted with handcraft shops, close the Spanish border.

Meanwhile, Coimbra, one of the best destinations to visit in Portugal for history and modern culture, beckons with medieval elegance. The old town, which is home to Portugal's oldest university, exudes old world charm and a liveliness generated by the student population, with plenty of opportunities to hear fado music – listening to this moving, melancholic traditional song accompanied by guitars is a highlight of any trip to Portugal.

Market rambles

Most major cities have a daily municipal market where you can buy fresh meat, fish, fruit, vegetables, and bread, which is typically supplemented by a larger weekly event where you can also buy clothes, shoes, ceramics, baskets, flowers, and a million other things you didn't think you needed. These markets provide an excellent opportunity to learn about Portuguese culture while also purchasing supplies and mementos to take home.

The best flea market in the country is Lisbon's Feira da Ladra (held on Tuesday and Saturday), while the small town of

Barcelos comes alive on Thursdays with one of Europe's best open-air marketplaces, which has been held since medieval times.

You've come to the correct place if you want to take home some loucas de Barçelos (local white and yellow ceramics), traditional basketry, and other crafts - it's a highlight of any vacation to Portugal.

From city thrills to surf breaks, here are ten of the best places to visit in Portugal.

Sintra seems like it came straight out of a fairytale.

Sintra, just a half-hour train ride from the capital, feels like another universe, and it's a terrific place to visit for a day trip away from the hustle and bustle of the metropolis. This medieval hillside township, dotted with stone-walled pubs and lorded over by a multicolored palace, looks like something out of a fairy tale. Imposing castles, magical gardens, weird homes, and centuries-old monasteries hidden among the trees create the backdrop to this fantasy environment. The fog that descends at night adds to the mystery; cold evenings are best spent in one of Sintra's many exquisite B&Bs, beside the fire.

Porto is a romantic city that will steal your heart.

It's difficult to imagine a more charming city than Porto. The tiny pedestrian streets, baroque churches, and spacious plazas of the country's second-largest municipality lead the eye south towards the Duoro River and its prominent bridges. There's no shortage of things to see and do, to say the least. Start in the Ribeira district, which is a UNESCO World Heritage Site, and then cross the bridge to Vila Nova de Gaia, where you may sample the world's best port. Modern architecture, cosmopolitan dining, dynamic nightlife, and cultural activity are infusing new life into Porto, which is characterized by its aura of dignified past.

Évora is a city that mixes medieval charm with youthful vigor.

Évora, the capital of the Alentejo province and one of Portugal's best-preserved medieval towns, is a charming destination to spend a few days. Narrow, meandering alleyways lead inside the 14th-century walls to remarkable antiquities such as an exquisite medieval cathedral and cloisters, Roman ruins, and a lovely town center. But Évora isn't just a dusty museum; it's also a bustling university town with a plethora of restaurants serving substantial Alentejan fare.

Lisbon is the place to go if you want to have a fun night out.

Lisbon's postcard-perfect picture of cobblestone alleyways, white-domed cathedrals, and large civic squares – a mesmerizing scene constructed over centuries – is viewed from seven renowned hills. The Portuguese capital is brimming with galleries to visit (including the fantastic Museu Coleço Berardo, which houses works by Hockney, Warhol, and Pollock), castles to visit (the hilltop Castelo de S Jorge being the most notable), and enough pastel de nata (custard tart) spots to satisfy even the sweetest visitor. Lisbon's nightlife, though, is its trump card, with a mix of old-school drinking dives, brassy jazz clubs, and open-all-night clubs that come alive once the sun sets.

In the Algarve, celebrate Portugal's diverse coastline.

When it comes to beaches in Portugal, sunseekers have a lot to be happy about. The Algarve, located on the south coast, is known for its beautiful and diverse shoreline. On the crowded sands of large resorts, you can join the crowds or enjoy coastal tranquility on stunning wild beaches surrounded by jagged cliffs. Days are spent playing in the waves, strolling along the beach, or surfing some of Europe's best waves. Summer brings endless days of sunlight and warm ocean temperatures, but you'll have to share the Algarve with a throng; if you prefer a more private experience, visit in the winter.

The only ski slope in Portugal is located in Parque Natural da Serra da Estrela.

For rough landscapes, outdoor adventures, and a dying traditional way of life, head to the Serra da Estrela, Portugal's highest mountain range. Hikers can pick from a network of high-country paths with breathtaking views, and charming mountain villages serve as excellent locations for outdoor pursuits. You can slalom down Portugal's only ski slope at the country's highest point, the peak of Torre, which was artificially pushed up to 2000m/6561ft by the erection of a not-so-subtle stone monument.

The best time to visit Portugal

With its magnificent natural beauty, hip cities, lovely towns, and incredible food, Portugal has something for everyone. Whatever your interests are, there is plenty to see and do in the Algarve, from the beaches to the whimsical enchantment of Sintra. During the sweltering summer months, expect crowds, while surfers can expect monster waves in the winter. The shoulder seasons of spring and fall may provide travelers with the best of both worlds. Is your unsure what time being best for you? The ideal time to visit Portugal is now.

High Season: July and August

Best time for warm ocean swimming

Ocean temperatures in the Algarve will be warmer if you're planning a beach holiday. There will, however, be a lot of people there, as well as other seaside tourist places.

Accommodation costs might skyrocket by up to 30% during the peak season. If you enjoy the heat, now is the best time to visit Portugal, as these are the hottest months of the year with scorching temperatures.

April to June and September to November

Best time for exploring the outdoors

Wildflowers and moderate days are great for treks and outdoor sports, allowing you to see some of Portugal's most beautiful natural sights. In June, there are a slew of exciting festivals to attend. The people and costs are typical, but the water temperature is significantly lower. It's also a wonderful time to visit cities like Lisbon and Porto when the crowds are thinner.

How to get around in Portugal

Trains or trams, 2 wheels or 4

By train

Portugal has a vast railway network that runs virtually the entire length of the country, making travel between destinations economical, pleasant, convenient, and often scenic. Trains run between popular tourist destinations including as Lisbon, Faro, Lagos, Porto, and Figueria da Foz, as well as international links to Madrid and Paris.

The majority of train services, which run from Faro in the south to Valença do Minho in the north, are classed as Regionais (R) or Interregionais (IR). The contemporary, high-speed Alfa Pendulares (AP) trains travel from Lisbon to Faro and from Lisbon to Braga via Santarém, Coimbra, Aveiro, and Porto. Intercidades (IC) are faster and more expensive services that connect Lisbon to the major regional centers. Urban services (urbanos) in Lisbon (to Cascais, Sintra, Setbal, and Vila Franca de Xira) and Porto (to Aveiro, Braga, and Guimares) offer a convenient commuting link to other towns, and both cities have an underground metro system.

On the timetables, international services are denoted as IN. Restaurant cars are only available on the Faro-Porto Comboio Azul and international trains like Sud-Expresso and Talgo Lusitânia, though all IC and Alfa trains provide aisle service and most have bars.

The cities of Lisbon and Porto each have their own urbano (suburban) train networks. Sintra, Cascais, Setbal, and the lower Tagus valley are all served by the Lisbon network. The network in Porto stretches as far as Braga, Guimares, and Aveiro, stretching the meaning of "suburban" to new heights. Between Coimbra and Figueira da Foz, there are additional urbano services.

Train tickets can be purchased on the official CP website or at stations across the country. Tickets for Intercidade and Alfa

Pendular can be reserved up to 30 days in advance, while seats for the next or even same day are usually available. Other services must be reserved at least 24 hours in advance.

Children under the age of five travel for free, while children aged five to twelve travel for half price. Additionally, with a valid ID, tourists aged 65 and up can receive a 50% discount on any service.

By bus

Almost all of the country's towns and villages are connected by buses, which are run by a variety of private companies. It can be perplexing at times: at some bus stations, two or more firms may operate services to the same towns; on the other hand, buses to the same destination may depart from various terminals. There is, however, a national network of express buses, with Rede Expressos providing daily service to locations around the country. Rodonorte in the north, Rodotejo in the Ribatejo, Rodoviária do Alentejo in the Alentejo, and EVA and Frota Azul in the Algarve are all important bus carriers.

Tickets can be purchased online or at bus stations and ticket counters (typically at cafés near the bus stop/station). It's a good idea to buy tickets ahead of time, but even in tourist locations in the summer, the day before is typically OK. The Lisbon–Porto express route and the Faro–Lisbon route both costs roughly €20. Under-4s travel free, under-13s half-price, and under-29s and senior citizens over 65 with proper documentation receive discounts.

Local and rural bus services go virtually everywhere you're likely to want to go, with the notable exception of remote beaches and some of the natural parks, including much of the Serra da Estrela, Serra de Malcata and Montesinho. Note, however, that services are often restricted to one or two departures a day, or geared towards school drop-offs/pickups and market times – meaning early-morning weekday departures, sometimes only during term times. Many local services are reduced – or nonexistent – at weekends.

By car

Exploring Portugal on two or four wheels is a wonderful way to experience the country because it allows you to roam freely without being restricted by public transportation. The country's highway network is constantly upgraded and expanded, with important roads paved and in generally good shape. Driving through Portugal's little walled towns, on the other hand, may be challenging, since roads can quickly thin to donkey-cart size and intricate one-way systems can force you off of your way. Renting a car in Portugal is reasonably simple, with rental agencies located in major cities, towns, and airports such as Lisbon, Porto, and Faro.

Rates in the Algarve are lower than elsewhere due to competition, and booking ahead will usually save you money. Amoita, Holiday Autos, and Europcar are just a few of the vehicle rental firms that operate in the country.

Motorcycles and scooters are available for rent in the bigger cities and along the coastal Algarve. A scooter/motorcycle will set you back between €30 and €60 per day.

To drive a car or motorcycle in Portugal, citizens of the EU, the United Kingdom, the United States, and Brazil just require their home driving license. Before embarking on any trip, others should obtain an International Driving Permit (IDP) in their home country.

Car safety belts are required to be worn in the front and back seats by law, and children under the age of 12 are not permitted to ride in the front. Motorcycle riders and passengers must wear helmets, and motorcycles must have working headlights at all times of the day and night. Driving while using a cell phone is likewise prohibited in Portugal.

Bicycle across gorgeous Portuguese scenery.

Cycling is popular in Portugal, despite the lack of designated bike paths. There are several itineraries to choose from in the north's hilly national and natural parks (particularly Parque

Nacional da Peneda-Gerês), along the coast, and over the Alentejo plains. Starting from the north and traveling south, following the prevailing winds, is the easiest way to travel down the coast. The Serra da Estrela (which acts as the Tour de Portugal's mountain run) is more difficult. Try the Serra do Maro, which runs between Amarante and Vila Real.

Be warned that cycling conditions aren't always ideal, with cobblestone streets in some historic towns liable to rattle your teeth loose if your tires aren't wide enough; city bikers should have wheels with a diameter of at least 38mm.

By tram, travel between Lisbon and Porto.

Taking a ride on one of Portugal's vintage trams has become a must-do activity in the country. These quaint rattling relics roll through the winding alleyways of Lisbon and Porto, providing a charming way to take an inexpensive sightseeing tour of both cities. Because word has gotten out, they can get very crowded during the summer, so get there early to obtain a good seat.

In Portugal, public transit is easily accessible.

Accessibility for disabled visitors to Portugal is somewhat limited. Private enterprises are not compelled to provide access and amenities for people with disabilities, unlike government offices and agencies. Some adapted rooms are available in newer and larger hotels, albeit the facilities may not be up to par; inquire at the local turismo. Most campgrounds provide handicapped-accessible restrooms, and some hostels have facilities for disabled guests.

The Lisbon airport is wheelchair accessible, and the airports of Porto and Faro feature wheelchair-accessible restrooms.

Parking

Many towns and beach resorts are increasingly clogged with traffic, especially during the summer, so finding a central parking space may be difficult. Park-and-ride services are available in some places, including as Coimbra, and large car parks are available at suburban metro stations in Porto. If you're looking for a parking spot in a city, follow the residents' lead and use the empty places that have been pointed out to you. Tipping the man who does the pointing €0.50 will compensate them for watching after your automobile. Even in the tiniest municipalities, on-street parking is frequently metered. The cost varies but averages €0.80 per hour on weekdays, Saturday afternoons, and all-day Sunday. It is normally free from 8 p.m. to 8 a.m. the next morning on weekdays, Saturday afternoons, and all-day Sunday.

Accessible Portugal, a Lisbon-based organization that promotes accessible tourism and is the brains behind the excellent TUR4all Portugal app, which acts as a database of accessible tourist resources and services throughout Portugal and Spain, and the Secretaria do Nacional de Reabilitaço, the national governmental organization that represents people with disabilities, are two useful resources for disabled travelers. The organization disseminates information, provides links to relevant services, and produces (in Portuguese) guides that provide recommendations for barrier-free lodging, transportation, stores, restaurants, and attractions.

CHAPTER THREE
15 Essential Dishes to Try in Portugal

The popularity of Portuguese food is on the rise. The small Iberian Nation That Could has finally shifted its focus inward in its pursuit of gastronomic validation after decades of turning toward the more well-known cuisines of its European sisters (France, Italy) as the apex of fine gastronomy. The Portuguese food renaissance, spearheaded by famous two-starred Michelin chefs José Avillez (Belcanto), Henrique Sá Pessoa (Alma), and Ricardo Costa (the Yeatman), started in Lisbon and Porto, two of Europe's hottest hotspots since Portugal recovered from the global recession, and quickly spread throughout this previously unnoticed maritime nation.

What is Portuguese cuisine?

The Age of Discovery, during which time Vasco de Gama and Pedro lvares Cabral sailed for the New World at the encouragement of Portuguese Prince Henry the Navigator in the 15th century, as well as Portugal's 1,115 miles of Atlantic coastline, had a significant impact on Portuguese cuisine.

Since seafood dominates Portuguese cuisine, hog holds its own in the interior. For instance, the robust regional food of the Alentejo is built on slow-cooked porco preto (Iberian black pig), lamb, and bread, all of which are prepared in various ways. Portuguese cuisine is supported by a lengthy range of traditional meals with Mediterranean roots that are served both on land and at sea. These recipes are seasoned with flavors from Africa, Brazil, and the Spice Route.

This multinational mashup has been developed into one of the most rigorous and vibrant cuisines on the continent by today's new culinary darling in Europe.

What is Portugal's most famous dish?

Salted cod, or bacalhau, won't be found in Portugal; rather, bacalhau will locate you. Bacalhau continued in Portugal despite technological developments, harkening back to a pre-refrigeration method of preserving fish in salt. Today, the majority of the bacalhau imported annually originates from Norway and weighs over 25,000 tons. Bacalhau can be either tasty or quite fishy depending on how it is prepared (some claim there are at least 1000 methods) (the trick is in extensive soaking in water to remove the salt). In either case, you won't be leaving the nation without tasting it.

Bacalhau can be grilled, cooked as a filet or in casseroles, baked with scrambled eggs, onions, and fried potatoes (bacalhau à

Brás, the most popular preparation and our favorite), or found floating in rice. Other noteworthy dishes are bacalhau à Gomes de Sá (cooked in the oven with potatoes, onion, garlic, and olive oil), bacalhau com natas, and bacalhau à Lagareiro (loin baked with olive oil and potatoes). In all honesty, every Portuguese restaurant in the nation excels at serving this particular dish, but Solar Do Bacalhau in Coimbra is regarded as one of the greatest.

1. **Pastel de nata (custard tart)**

Portuguese egg tarts, a little and indulgent delicacy that some could argue is the most satisfying wallop of sweet, sweet wow you'll ever get for €1.15, are the nation's most well-known dessert. Even if you know almost nothing about Portuguese food, you're probably familiar with it. It is protected as pastel de Belém at Antiga Confeitaria de Belém, where it is supposed to have started in the Lisbon suburbs in 1837 and is popularly known as pastel de nata globally. The UNESCO-listed Jerónimos Monastery in the area passed down the original recipe, which is now secret. However, the key lies in the tactile contrast between the flaky pastry crust and the creamy egg custard filling.

2. Bifanas

There aren't many sandwiches that can compare to the bifana in terms of taste. This traditional Portuguese meal gets its kick from the thin slices of pork that have been marinated for hours in a delicious mixture of white wine, paprika, garlic, and other spices. And the combo is exquisite when it's served in a soft or crunchy bread roll with mustard! Want to turn it into a whole meal? You're set if you add some french fries to the side.

The bifana is a dish that is popular throughout Portugal, although the traditional version is thought to have originated in Vendas Novas, a town close to Lisbon.

3. Sardinhas assadas (grilled sardines)

The Portuguese summer may bring sunshine and clear sky, but the forecast is never guaranteed to be favorable. However, throughout the summer holiday season, historic neighborhoods around Lisbon (and abroad) are filled with the seductive smell of grilling sardines. From June through October, when they are at their plumpest and tastiest, freshly grilled sardines are widely available, beginning with the celebrations of Santo António, one of Portugal's most popular saints (outside of that period, they are likely to have been frozen).

The preparation is straightforward, as is typical for the best foods: Sardines are typically served with a piece of broa (corn bread) or, in restaurants, with traditional sides like bell pepper salad and boiled potatoes (although they're always best eaten in the street next to a neighborhood grill). Sardines are typically served coarsely salted and grilled over hot coals. Visit O Pitéu in Graça in Lisbon, a restaurant that has served traditional Portuguese food for more than 30 years.

4. Francesinha ("Little Frenchie")

Portugal's "Little Frenchie" scores way too high on the ridiculousness scale to be considered food for humans: A mouthwatering combination of wet cured ham, linguiça sausage, steak or roast beef, melting cheese, and occasionally a fried egg atop thick bread drenched in a scalding tomato and beer sauce (and served with french fries, of course). It is the pride of Porto, a one-and-done gastronomic caravan of everything that is bad and amazing about a local delicacy, and at the same time a hangover cure and a ticket to the emergency room. Of course it's great.

Its name gives away its origins: Portuguese immigrants to France apparently boasted, "Segura a minha cerveja!" ("Hold my beer!") to their French friends and created the Francesinha in order to compete with that country's famous croque monsieur. Although there is considerable competition and disagreement among Porto residents, Lado B is frequently hailed as the best variant for beginners. Prepare to move quickly and wait for your plated fare because the hip café is often busy.

5. Queijo (cheese)

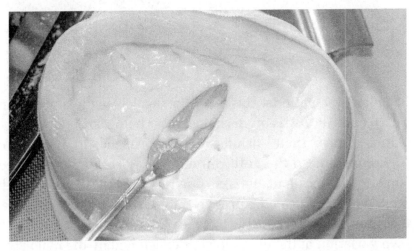

Portuguese cheeses are less well-known than other European cheeses, which is a good thing for Portugal because this little dairy paradise has countless types to explore. Try the creamy Azeito, an unpasteurized sheep's milk cheese from the foothills of the Arrábida Mountains south of Lisbon, the buttery Serra de Estrela, a sheep's milk cheese made in (and named after) Portugal's greatest mountain range, and the semi-soft, peppery So Jorge from the Azores.

6. Bacalhau

Bacalhau, the national cuisine of Portugal, is made of dried and salted codfish that is often cooked after being soaked in milk or water. Since their fishing boats brought it back from Newfoundland in the 16th century, the Portuguese have been consuming bacalhau. It is so well-liked that it goes by the moniker "loyal friend," or fiel amigo. In addition, the locals even make reference to it in folk songs. Each location has its own variation of the dish, which is consumed by the majority of residents at least once a week.

7. Caldo verde

In Portugal, a soup dish is a staple of most meals. Even though cold tomato soups, fish, and bread are quite popular, the caldo verde from northern Portugal's Minho Province is the most well-known. Only five ingredients are often used to make this comforting green soup: potato, onion, kale that has been finely sliced, olive oil, and chorizo sausage. This national favorite can be found practically anywhere in Portugal; from the hippest restaurants in Lisbon to the far-flung farmhouses in the villages. It is filling, affordable, and the ideal comfort meal. It pairs well with broa, a soft-textured Portuguese cornmeal that has a crusty exterior.

8. Cataplana de Marisco

A traditional fish or shellfish stew known as cataplana de marisco gets its name from the clam-shaped copper pot of the same name. When the Moors came to Portugal from North Africa in the seventh century, they brought the dish with them. The Algarve's national dish is cataplana. Although the ingredients differ depending on the region, they typically include white fish, shellfish, red peppers, onions, and a small amount of chile. All of this is combined inside the cataplana, and the lid is securely fastened before it is steam-cooked to perfection. Rice, fries, or fresh crusty bread go best with this delectable stew.

9. Cozido à Portuguesa

For meat lovers, you just must taste this traditional Portuguese stew. In spite of the fact that cozido à Portuguesa is available all across the nation in a variety of regional varieties, it typically includes beef, pork, chicken, and various smoked sausages including morcela, chouriço, alheira, and farinheira. Along with potatoes, carrots, and cabbage, it can also include various other animal parts, such as a pig's ear or foot. The various ingredients are added at various times and cooked together in a single pot. As a result, a delicious and rich dish is produced, which the Portuguese revere as a national treasure and a part of their legacy.

10. Leitão assado da bairrada

Porco Preto and other forms of pork are prevalent in Portuguese cuisine (Iberian black pig). It is raised free-range, frequently on an acorn diet, and is mostly found in the central and southern regions. Pork that has been produced is moist and sweet-tasting, and it can be cooked, grilled, pickled, and added to bread and soups. Leito assado da bairrada, or roast suckling pig, is the mother of all Portuguese pork recipes. This can be found on menus across the nation. Traditionally, coarse salt and pepper are used to season the pig's skin before it is impaled on a stick and smeared with a mixture of garlic and pig grease. Then it is roasted and basted until the crisp, golden-orange skin is achieved and the highly flavorful flesh begins to fall off the bone. Typically, you'll have it with lettuce, tomato, and onion salad along with batatas fritas (fries) (salada mista).

11. Pastéis de nata

Pastéis de nata is a popular Portuguese custard tart that is small, circular, and totally delicious. Crisp puff pastry cups filled with egg custard and dusted with cinnamon and powdered sugar make up this famous dish. Pastéis de nata were invented at the Jerónimos Monastery in Lisbon's Santa Maria de Belém district. Egg whites were once used by monks to starch their clothing, and the leftover yolks were subsequently utilized to bake cakes and pastries. When the monastery, along with all the other convents and monasteries in Portugal, was liquidated in 1834, they sold the formula to the close-by sugar plant. In 1837, the business began baking the renowned Pastéis de Belém, and it still does today. These delectable tarts may be found in bakeries in Macau and all around Portugal. Warm, directly from the oven, is when they taste the best.

12. Arroz doce

Portuguese people have a sweet tooth, therefore there are many tasty treats to choose from in the neighborhood bakeries and pastry stores. Local desserts are all rich and sweet, frequently egg-based and occasionally creamy. It is typical to eat creamy, egg-based desserts with cinnamon and vanilla flavors as well at the end of a meal. Be sure to try arroz doce, a classic Portuguese rice pudding, and leite crème, an egg custard with a firm caramel topping akin to crème brûlée. This comforting, sweet, and creamy delicacy is always flavored with lemon and cinnamon but can also be made with egg or condensed milk.

13. Frango no churrasco

Frango no churrasco, a popular fast meal in Portugal, is literally translated as chicken on the grill. Another name for it is frango no brasa, which translates to chicken on burning embers. All around Portugal, you may order this delectable snack to go from little roadside stalls. But don't expect it to taste like KFC because this delicious treat is anything but fast food. It is prepared in a certain manner and served with delectable marinades developed from family recipes. Spatchcocked whole tiny chickens are then marinated in a mixture of white wine, paprika, lemon, and olive oil. Then they are placed over a coal pit on a spinning spit.

The marinade and the well-known Portuguese piri piri chile sauce are continuously baste the birds while they roast to maintain their juicy texture. The smoky, spicy, sweet chicken is then typically served with fries, salad, bread, or rice and a lovely cold bottle of beer.

14. Francesinha

In Porto, numerous eateries offer their own interpretations of this traditional Portuguese cuisine classic, but this upgraded sandwich reigns supreme. This meal, a culinary classic, frequently starts with thick layers of ham, sausage, cheese, roast meat, and other regional specialties. In light of this, there are many inventive and delectable versions.

15. Polvo à lagareiro

If you enjoy eating octopus, you'll be happy to know that the Portuguese have mastered the technique for making it flavorful and soft. In this recipe, the octopus is first boiled before being roasted with potatoes in the oven. When it comes to traditional Portuguese cuisine, this is a true delight, finished with a good dose of olive oil.

CHAPTER FOUR

Where to Stay in Portugal: Best Places & Hotels

Portugal is a beautiful country with delicious food, a vibrant culture, and a long history. In this exciting and diverse country, there is so much to see and do, and there is a destination to suit every tourist. There are green island getaways, medieval hilltop capitals, and multicultural urban towns, not to mention its beautiful coastline. In this country that gets plenty of sun, there is something for everyone.

There is much to see and do in Portugal's charming cities, many of which feature historical districts brimming with intriguing buildings and mouthwatering restaurants. The best place to start your exploration of the Portuguese countryside is one of the cities, many of which are surrounded by picturesque villages and landscapes.

The cost of hotels and other accommodations is frequently quite low, and they offer excellent service. It is simple to understand why more and more people are falling in love with Portugal when affordable public transportation and walkable city streets are added.

Lisbon

Lisbon is a stunning, endearing, and energetic city with a blend of ancient and contemporary structures. You will never run out of things to do in the Portuguese capital because there is so much to see and do there. Take advantage of the vibrant food scene, discover the riches of culture, and spend your evenings getting swept up in the vibrant nightlife.

Lisbon has a warm temperature all year long, making it one of Europe's most alluring cities, so it's strange that there aren't more tourists there. But it is simpler to explore the city when there aren't as many visitors. Base yourself close to the historic center, where there are many hotels to pick from and it's simple to go around the main attractions on foot, since this is the ideal location for a long weekend getaway.

Where to Stay in Lisbon

Luxury

Hotel Altis Avenida - This opulent 5-star hotel is housed in a historic structure that showcases the best of time-honored Portuguese architecture and interiors with Art Deco influences and is only a short distance from the renowned shopping triangle. The renowned Chef Joo Rodrigues runs the award-winning restaurant of the Altis Avenida Hotel, which has a breathtaking view of the Tagus river. The luxurious rooms here feature a dedicated desk and recognizable retro-style furniture.

Midrange

Figueira Beautique Hotels - This lovely 4-star hotel, created by the renowned interior designer Nini Andrade e Silva, is only a short distance from the illustrious Rossio Train Station. Among the amenities you can use while staying here are a specialized restaurant serving some of the greatest Portuguese cuisine, a vibrant bar, and a front desk open around-the-clock. The luxurious guestrooms have a unique design with fig tree accents and natural colors. A daily breakfast buffet is furthermore provided by Beautique Hotels Figueira.

Albufeira

The beachfront resort town of Albufeira, located along the Algarve coastline, is a bustling and active place with a wide variety of beaches. The town itself has developed throughout time, going from a small fishing village to a thriving vacation spot with a ton of lodging options, dining establishments, and, of course, vacationers.

The biggest resort town along this length of coastline is Albufeira, where the majority of the lodging options and points of interest are concentrated around the boisterous strip that is home to several bars and clubs. The lovely old town, with its whitewashed structures and little cobblestone roads, is a pleasant alternative for those seeking a more tranquil vacation.

Where to Stay in Albufeira

Luxury

Atlantico, Sao Rafael - The Sao Rafael Atlantico, a captivating 5-star resort with stunning views and exclusive access to So Rafael Beach, is unquestionably one of the best hotels in the area. This opulent resort has all the amenities you could want for a wonderful getaway, including three heated outdoor and indoor pools, a first-rate spa, and a buffet dining area. The rooms offer spectacular garden or ocean views and have a basic decor with gentle hues.

Midrange

The Sol e Mar Hotel This impressive 4-star hotel, just a few meters from Peneco Beach, is a great option for both leisure and business tourists. The Hotel Sol e Mar offers a number of interesting restaurants with stunning views and exquisite meals, as well as live entertainment most evenings. Other amenities and services offered at the hotel include a sizable indoor pool. The guestrooms at this hotel have ensuite bathrooms and satellite TV, and they also have unmatched sea views.

Porto

Porto is renowned across the world for its Port wine and is the ideal location for a city break. The city's history is extensive and varied, and it was significant to Portugal's past. This city's streets are steeped in history, notably Riberia, which is known for its old structures and winding streets.

Although visiting Porto isn't complete without trying the city's famous Port wine, there are a lot of other worthwhile attractions as well. Although the metro is accessible and reasonably priced, it is simple to get around on foot and take in the sights. There are many hotels to select from, and they frequently provide excellent value for the money.

Where to Stay in Porto

Luxury

Hotel Porto Palacio & Spa - This gorgeous 5-star hotel is a great option for luxury guests because it has a squash court, a top-notch spa with private massage rooms, and an indoor pool.

Porto Palácio Hotel & Spa is adorned with a rooftop patio that provides breathtaking views of Porto and the Douro River. It also includes a fantastic gym for fitness fanatics. The rooms here boast a modern design with wood furniture and soft colors. Additionally, they get a marble bathroom with underfloor heating and dual vanity units.

Midrange

European Stars Das Arts - This eccentric 4-star hotel is close to some of the most important local cultural organizations and is a fascinating blend of a modern structure and a historic structure. The guestrooms feature with a work desk and an ensuite bathroom, as well as hardwood floors and elegant furnishings. The amenities include a fantastic restaurant with a daily breakfast menu, a well maintained garden area, and a bustling bar. Rotating art shows are another feature of the hotel.

Funchal

The capital of Madeira is a contemporary metropolis that has grown more well-known in recent years for its great food scene. It is situated in a natural amphitheater. Funchal, which was formerly a rural community, has undergone extensive reconstruction and is now a charming city with sunshine all year round and a large number of hotels.

Funchal is a sheltered city that is brimming with beautiful flowers, nestled between magnificent mountains and the azure of the Atlantic coast. Being able to navigate the city on foot is common because of how safe it is. Beaches and water sports, as well as the delectable local food, are the focal points of many of the city's activities.

Where to Stay in Funchal

Luxury

The Cliff Bay - PortoBay - The breathtaking Cliff Bay 5-star resort, which is perched on a natural peninsula, provides you with both private access to the Atlantic Ocean and an outstanding view of it. The beautiful resort redefines luxury and splendor with a bevy of opulent amenities like a 2-Michelin star restaurant, multiple pools, an ultra-modern spa and wellness center, and a library. Each guestroom has two twin queen beds, a marble bathroom, and a private balcony.

Midrange

Hotel Santa Maria TURIM - This magnificent 4-star hotel is tastefully furnished and away from the city's busy hums, making it a great choice for both leisure and business tourists. An on-site restaurant and bar, a reputable business center, a shared lounge, and many other amenities and services are available here. Expect to be treated to a sumptuous breakfast spread each morning when staying in one of the many exquisite rooms here.

Lagos

Lagos is a well-liked vacation destination because it has a rich history, wonderful beaches, and a vibrant nightlife. The town, which is located along the Western Algarve Coast, has expanded from its historic core, which is teeming with stores, eateries, and bars and is the perfect place to base yourself while visiting the area. Hotels a bit outside of town are excellent options for people who enjoy beach life.

The busiest times of the year are the summer months, so plan ahead and reserve your lodging. You don't have to worry about crowds because to the abundance of beaches in the vicinity. Take a road trip down the coast in a car that you hired for the purpose of discovering the many beaches and the picturesque surroundings.

Where to Stay in Lagos

Lagos, Vila Gale - This lovely 4-star resort is all you need to unwind and have a revitalizing vacation in the middle of absolute tranquillity. It is located along the sparkling Meia

Praia Beach. A large outdoor and indoor pool, a landscaped garden, a fine dining restaurant, and a spa and wellness center with sauna, steam room, and massage facilities are just a few of the luxurious features and services offered at Vila Gale Lagos. The most cutting-edge audiovisual equipment is in every space, which has been creatively created.

Portimao

The ancient fishing and boat building industries have been replaced by the tourism industry in Portimao, a former industrial city. Many visitors come to this town to take advantage of the pleasant weather and to explore the charming city streets. There is a lot to do in the city, from amazing pedestrianized commercial areas to fascinating historical places; using public transportation is a pretty simple way to get around.

The majority of the town's hotels are located along the charming beachfront. Enjoy the abundance of eateries serving fresh seafood during your visit to the city, and then stroll the streets while taking in the laid-back, informal environment.

Where to Stay in Portimao

Hotel Jupiter Algarve - The Jupiter Algarve Hotel, which is located on the oceanfront in Portimo, has a stunning view of Praia da Rocha Beach. The 4-star hotel features an ocean-themed interior with outstanding amenities like a heated pool, spa and wellness areas, live entertainment, and a fine-dining restaurant with Portuguese and international cuisine and a live culinary station. There is a minibar and an ensuite bathroom in every hotel room. Some even have their own balcony.

Sintra

The charming village of Sintra is located in the Serra de Sintra hills. Because the town was well-liked by the Portuguese elite who constructed gorgeous palaces and rich homes here in the 19th century, the area is a draw for tourists who are interested in history and architecture. People who like to spend time in nature will love the pine-covered hills that hug the environment. There are numerous opportunities for trekking and rock climbing within the Parque Natural de Sintra-Cascais, which includes the little town.

Sintra, despite its modest size, is accustomed to tourists; numerous groups of day trippers arrive frequently. However, the best way to really experience Sintra's enticing ambience is to stay in one of the town hotels located in old structures.

Where to Stay in Sintra

Sintra's Vila Gale - This magnificent 5-star hotel delights you with first-rate service and cutting-edge amenities as it is situated in a gorgeous setting surrounded by lush vegetation. Vila Gale Sintra has a full-service spa with a Turkish bath, a number of rituals and therapies, and a heated indoor pool with a million-dollar view that was especially created to provide you with an intensive wellness experience. The hotel's distinctively themed rooms guarantee the utmost in luxury and comfort.

Aveiro

It's easy to see why Aveiro is frequently referred to as the "Venice of Portugal." The old city, best known for its crescent-shaped Moliceiros boats and decorative Art Nouveau architecture, is laced with canals and waterways. A lovely fishing community and magnificent churches are only a couple of the city's many historical attractions. There are many things to do in this city by the lake, including dining in one of the many restaurants, taking a boat tour, or just having a leisurely stroll around the charming streets.

The town has a variety of lodging options to fit various travel needs and budgets, and because to its proximity to the Porto urban train, getting into the city is a breeze. As an alternative, renting a car will provide you the opportunity to visit the nearby towns and beaches.

Where to Stay in Aveiro

Aveiro Palace Hotel This four-star hotel is housed in a historic structure constructed in 1937 and offers an unrivaled view of two of Aveiro's most well-known attractions. The luxurious features and services offered by Hotel Aveiro Palace are all created to live up to its illustrious past. Among the benefits of staying here are a chic common area, a restaurant with an old-fashioned tiled wall, and an educational breakfast buffet. The vibrant, soundproof guest rooms have parquet floors, an ensuite bathroom, and an ensuite bathtub.

Ponta Delgada

The vibrant capital of Sao Miguel, the largest island in the Azores, is Ponta Delgada. Pretty cobblestone streets in the city are lined with charming white-washed homes that conceal charming churches and intimate squares. What once was a sleepy fishing town has grown into a bustling metropolis where tourists can enjoy live music in the city's many restaurants and strolling along the seafront promenade.

The region's abundance of beautiful natural beauty is perfect for tourists who enjoy exploring. The town has numerous cozy hotels, and getting around on foot is easy. As an alternative, you can board a nearby bus to get where you're going.

Where to Stay in Ponta Delgada

Grand Hotel Atlantico - This spectacular 5-star hotel, which just underwent renovation, overlooks the marina in Ponta Delgada and is a luxury and business traveler's delight. Grand Hotel Açores Atlântico is all about comfort and tranquility. It has eight meeting rooms, a restaurant with a Portuguese-inspired menu, a year-round exhibit on maritime transportation, and a heated indoor pool. The minibar-equipped rooms in the European design include views of the city, the harbor, or both. Additionally, there is a regular breakfast spread with the finest locally grown foods.

CHAPTER FIVE

10 Best Beach Resorts in Portugal

If wading through waves washing up on beaches with golden sand is your notion of the ideal vacation, consider Portugal. Some of Europe's top beaches are located in this little Iberian Peninsula nation. A wet suit may be necessary if you plan to swim or surf in the Atlantic Ocean. The weather is finest in the summer months, although it is still possible to visit outside of the peak travel period. There are so many things to do at beach resorts in Portugal that you might need to return home to recover from your trip.

1. Martinhal Beach Resort

There are so many things to do at the Martinhal Beach Resort & Hotel that you might not have time to enjoy your elegantly furnished accommodation. Kite- and wind-surfing, kayaking, surfing, golf, fitness classes, tennis, and diving are just a few of the activities on the list. Face painting, cooking workshops, treasure hunts, and surfing lessons are just a few of the kid-friendly pursuits that will keep your kids entertained. Sagres, beaches with fine sand, and a natural park are all around the resort.

2. Praia D'El Rey Marriott

You can choose between ocean or golf course views when you stay at the elegantly designed Praia D'El Rey Marriott Golf & Beach Resort in Obidos. A championship 18-hole golf course is located on the resort. A short stroll will take you to the beach. There are four restaurants at the Marriott that each provide a distinct cuisine if you start to feel peckish. The closest airport is 70 kilometers (45 miles) away, and the hotel does not offer shuttle service, so you will need to make your own travel arrangements to get here.

3. VidaMar Resort Hotel Madeira

The VidaMar Resort Hotel Madeira is situated in a distinctive area: close to Funchal, the main island's city. The resort offers views of Funchal Bay. In fact, this upmarket hotel's 300 rooms all have views of the water, and the decor is kept simple to enhance these views. The resort has immediate access to the coast and is surrounded by tropical plants. Three swimming pools are available at the hotel, one of which is unheated for kids. Five restaurants are available for dining.

4. Crowne Plaza Vilamoura

The Crowne Plaza Vilamoura looms over the beach at Villamoura with its 12 stories of height. You are guaranteed a view since each of the 327 guest rooms has a balcony. Additionally, customers gush about how immaculately clean the wicker-accented rooms are. Although the beach is crowded with lounge chairs and umbrellas, the Crowne Plaza Vilamoura features three swimming pools, including one lagoon pool that is especially big and one that is just for kids. Your children will like the playground there as well. There are two eateries on the property.

5. Memmo Baleeira Hotel

The Memmo Baleeira Hotel has a light, airy vibe to it because to its all-white structures, which contrast wonderfully with the surrounding greenery, golden sand, and blue ocean. It is situated in Sagres, one of the top surfing destinations in Europe, and the hotel features a surf school on site that instructs beginners how to catch waves. Baleeira's fishing village is visible from some of the 144 apartments' balconies. Fresh fish is the restaurant's specialty, and also serves Mediterranean cuisine.

6. Pestana Palm Gardens

If you choose to stay with Pestana Palm Gardens for your Portuguese beach vacation, they guarantee you will have the time of your life. There is little doubt that from its perch atop a cliff overlooking the ocean, this four-star resort in Carvoeiro offers breath-taking vistas. With regard to amenities, there are well-kept gardens, a tennis court, outdoor swimming pools (one of which is kid-friendly), and table tennis. Two world-class golf courses are just ten minutes apart by car. At Vale do Covo, the distance to the beach is three minutes. There are balconies or terraces in guest rooms.

7. Cascade Wellness & Lifestyle Resort

A tranquil atmosphere can be found at the Cascade Wellness & Lifestyle Resort, which has views of the Atlantic Ocean. Its activities are made to help you unwind even more. Tennis courts, numerous swimming pools, a fitness facility with guided workouts, and full spa services are available. Although you can stroll to the beach, visitors advise you'll need a car to travel to Lagos, the closest town, to shop and eat. The hotel's shuttle service is also not always available, and one restaurant only serves dinner while the other is only open during certain times of the year.

8. Tivoli Carvoeiro

As it is perched on a cliff overlooking Vale do Covo in the Algarve, Tivoli Carvoeiro offers breathtaking views of the surrounding area. The resort structure itself has the appearance of having been carved out of a cliff. Early in 2017, the hotel underwent a significant refurbishment; one outcome was fewer but larger guest rooms. Although the resort has views of the Atlantic Ocean, it is difficult for walkers to get to the beach; instead, the resort suggests four beaches that are accessible by car.

9. Vilalara Thalassa Resort

Vilalara Thalassa Resort is the place to go if you enjoy your seclusion. There is a gated entry to this resort with five-star apartments and suites. The verdant garden backdrop also enhances the sense of seclusion. Four tennis courts and four outdoor saltwater pools are available at the resort. Here, health is prioritized. One of the top Thalassotherapy facilities in the world is located at Vilalara Thalassa Resort, which also provides other wellness services. Low-calorie food is served even at the restaurant.

10.Pestana Dom Joao II

Among the best hotels in the Algarve is Pestana Dom Joao II. A large part of this is due to its location on the long, winding beach of Alvor. The town center can be reached by foot in 10 minutes from the hotel and is only a few feet away from the beach. The outdoor pool is saltwater filled and offers a variety of water sports like pedal boats and diving. One restaurant, three bars—one of which is open all year—and a hotel make up the Portuguese resort.

5 Best Day Trips in Portugal
1. Day Trip from Lisbon to Sintra and Cascais

Besides being a great starting point for day trips elsewhere, Lisbon is a lively city in Portugal. You may visit Sintra and Cascais on a day trip from Lisbon, which will take you by picturesque mountains, castles, and surfers while passing seaside landscapes.

The amazing day starts in the Portuguese capital, where you'll board an air-conditioned minivan for the short 30-minute trip from Lisbon to Sintra. Sintra is exceptional because it has both rich estate homes from more recent eras and world-class sceneries and landscapes, in addition to medieval palaces. It is easy to understand why so many affluent and regal individuals have resided in this region of Portugal: it is breathtakingly gorgeous! Take a stroll around Pena Park's paths, then proceed to the Pena National Palace to see it for yourself.

The palace is located at the summit of Sintra Mountain and features opulent interior design from the 19th century. You will have some free time to eat lunch in Sintra or take a tour of the historic Sintra National Palace after exploring the interior of the opulent palace.

In order to get to Sintra National Park, we briefly return to the minivan. The drive passes recognizable monuments like the Palace of Monserrate, so keep an eye out the window. You will be standing near to Cabo da Roca in the national park, which is Europe's westernmost point and a rugged bluff. At Guincho

Beach, observe local surfers catching waves before traveling to Cascais.

The ideal area to take a barefoot stroll in the beach while watching the waves crash against the shore of this classic Portuguese fishing village is in the little coastal town of Cascais. Take pictures of the famous white homes with terra-cotta roofs that are arranged in a row just steps from the Atlantic Ocean before you depart. Enjoy the unobstructed views of the picturesque town of Estoril as you go back to Lisbon.

2. Day Tour from Porto to Douro Valley with River Cruise

If you're visiting Porto, you're probably well aware of the city's status as a major wine producing region. If all you're drinking is the local port, though, you might be losing out. You can take a trip from Porto to the Douro Valley to take in the magnificent landscape that surrounds Porto and to sample some of the other world-class wines that Portugal is renowned for.

The tour of a wine enthusiast starts in Porto, where you board a cozy minivan and go to Pinho. You can stop for a quick photo opportunity in Peso da Régua, the capital of the Douro Valley, halfway there. You will have the ability to independently explore Pinho once you've gotten there. Don't miss the famous Pinho train station, which was constructed in 1937 and features blue and white tiles, many of which feature locals and natural environment. You may also see the amazing bridge that was constructed by none other than Gustave Eiffel, the same designer of the Eiffel Tower in Paris, France.

A leisurely cruise down the Douro River is the next activity on the schedule. As you board a traditional rabelo, one of the community's cargo boats, you'll pass some gorgeous estates, wineries, and vineyards that are situated along the river. After the river tour, it's time for lunch in a neighborhood villa and a drink of Douro Valley wine.

The afternoon itinerary includes two more family-run wine properties where you may learn about the area's winemaking process. There will be plenty of opportunity for you to sample the local port as well as the other red and white wines that are available. You might even wish to buy a few bottles to bring home as a memento. You return to the city in time for your dinner reservations after the return trip to Porto.

3. Day Trip from Lisbon to Fatima, Nazare and Obidos

You may discover a whole different aspect of Portugal that extends beyond the busy metropolis on this unforgettable day trip from Lisbon. You may visit wonderful religious monuments, historical buildings, fishing villages, and stunning landscapes all in one day.

The day starts in Lisbon, where small groups of no more than 15 depart for Fátima in air-conditioned minivans. Fátima is a significant Christian pilgrimage place and is around 130 kilometers (80 miles) from Lisbon. Since 1917, when three shepherd children encountered the saintly Lady of Fatima, this day has been commemorated by pilgrimages to Fátima. The amazing Basilica of Fátima, a stunning cathedral that receives millions of visitors a year, is the final stop. The Batalha Monastery, built in the 14th century and featuring incredibly elaborate Gothic architecture, is the next site.

The next stop, Nazare, is only a short drive away from there. Portuguese people adore visiting this seaside town, and many of them do so to enjoy the beach throughout the summer. Spend some time on your own to choose lunch, which should absolutely include some of the delicious regional seafood readily available at many of the beach restaurants. Reunite with the group, take in the view from the Nazare cliffs, and then start out on a stroll to the unassuming yet charming settlements of So Martinho do Porto and Foz do Arelho.

There is one more stop before reaching Lisbon: bidos. An astounding 2,200 years have passed since the founding of this medieval town. It is possible to enjoy amazing vistas of the medieval defended walls, winding lanes built before cars were common, and surprisingly vibrant homes thanks to the town's truly ancient architecture. Before you leave, finish your vacation with a sip of the Ginja liqueur, a traditional cherry alcoholic beverage.

4. Guimarães and Braga Day Trip from Porto

For this day trip, you leave Porto and travel a short distance to Guimares and Braga, where you will spend the entire day experiencing their cultures. The ancient past is incredibly rich in these two cities in northern Portugal. You may study about the Palace of the Dukes of Braganza and see the Guimares Castle from the tenth century here.

Following your time spent learning about the past, you'll stop for lunch at a nearby restaurant where you'll have a mouthwatering traditional two-course Portuguese meal. When you've had your fill, spend an afternoon learning about Roman history with an informed guide.

History enthusiasts should definitely take this tour. One of the first Christian cities in Portugal, Braga is renowned for its religious legacy and has a large number of churches and other religious structures. Nevertheless, the Bom Jesus do Monte, a stunning neoclassical church, is what makes it so well-known.

You can also explore Braga on foot. This is a wonderful chance to take in attractions like its magnificent Baroque church and a museum devoted to religious art. Aside from its history, this city is filled with vibrant streets because of its student population.

5. Évora Day Trip from Lisbon

Those who wish to try some of the local cuisine and flavors should definitely do this day trip. By leaving the Portuguese capital and traveling across the Vasco da Gama bridge to the other side of the Tagus River on an excursion to discover the old Roman city of Évora, you can really make the most of your time in the Mediterranean.

Another historical site, this one is known for the 16th-century St. Francis Church. It's a bit of a morbid attraction because it features a chapel filled with endless rows of human skulls. There is also the magnificent Cathedral of Évora. Then, take a moment to awe at the Roman Temple remains, which date all the way back to the first century AD.

The main plaza of Évora, Giraldo Square, is the next stop. It is bustling with activity and surrounded by rows of stunning old buildings, as well as the essential cafes for when you need a pick-me-up and a delectable local snack. Since the square's erection in the 1570s, its appearance and mood have remained unchanged.

You'll be taken to sample some incredibly delectable olive oil by your knowledgeable, local tour guide. The good stuff is made here according to a long tradition. A wonderful opportunity to learn—and taste, of course! And a stop at the Almendres Cromlech archaeological site on the way back to Lisbon. Over 6,000 years ago, these enormous standing stones were erected here and were used to calculate the equinoxes and solstices.

CHAPTER SIX

Best Things to Do with Kids in Lisbon

Lisbon offers a ton of family-friendly activities and tourist sites to keep children busy while exploring. The magnificent Oceanário de Lisboa, which is situated near Parque das Nacoes, is one of the city's most well-liked attractions. The astounding variety of marine life housed in this first-rate institution will wow both parents and children. Castelo de So Jorge is another attraction that should be on everyone's itinerary because it is certain to occupy children of all ages for hours. They are free to roam the gardens, play on the ramparts (with parental supervision), and take in the breathtaking cityscapes. All kids enjoy going to zoos, and the city's fascinating Jardim Zoológico has unique white tigers among its residents that are eager to meet kids.

1. OCEANARIO DE LISBOA

You may understand why kids are drawn to this top-notch tourist attraction by listening to the pretend screams of fright as the sharks pass by. Children are completely enthralled by the astounding array of marine life on exhibit at Europe's second-largest aquarium. Amazingly, the oceanarium is home to over 8000 distinct aquatic species, and in addition to sharks, there are a number of ray species and one or two surprises, such the adorably calm sunfish, to inspire admiration and awe.

Away from the main tank, marine life is abundant and incredibly diversified. Keep an eye out for the delicate sea dragons and the vibrant angelfish! The two sea otters that enchant the crowds with their adorable antics and playfulness, however, receive the loudest collective oohs and arrhs. This attraction makes for a special family outing because it is both entertaining and educational in equal measure.

2. CASTELO DE SAO JORGE

Every child enjoys a castle, and the larger the better. Fortunately, Lisbon Castle is one of the largest in the nation, and children can experience a pretend world of medieval fantasy there. In a location like this, the mind can go wild. The castle walls provide envious views of downtown Lisbon in addition to the archaeological site and the remnants of the ancient royal Alcáçova mansion situated within the grounds. Visit the Tower of Ulysses for a close-up view, where a camera obscura offers a 360-degree panorama of the city below in real time. The grounds are large, and among the umbrella pine, cork oak, olive, and carob trees, it's simple to get lost. Visit the castle café for tea and cake if you need some food or a spot to rest.

3. JARDIM ZOOLOGICO

The Lisbon Zoo attracts youthful, inquisitive minds. Children can spend countless hours here learning about the incredibly broad range of species that calls the zoo home. A family of spectacular mountain gorillas and a rare and stunning white tiger are among the local inhabitants. Numerous primates from all over the world astonish with their exuberant activities, but the sleek dolphins and sea lions frequently steal the show, especially when they're being fed. Children can have pleasure exploring the enchanted woodland and counting how many birds they can find. Additionally, there is a separate children's farm where younger children can interact with adorable domestic animals. The zoo's layout is an experience in and of itself.

A cable car winds its way through the lush canopy above the enclosures, including the interesting reptile house, while a train winds its way around them all. The imagination is further stimulated by an amusement park.

4. HIPPOTRIP

Hippotrip uses an amphibious custom-built vehicle to explore the city center before moving on to Belem to drive down a ramp at the harbor and into the River Tagus. It is unquestionably the most innovative tourist option now offered in Lisbon. It's an exciting land-sea experience that will appeal to anyone with a spirit of adventure and who enjoys trying new things. The bus travels to locations including Praça do Comércio and Jardim da Estrela after leaving Doca de Santo Amaro in the city's Alcântara neighborhood. Later, it drives by the famous Jerónimos monastery before slamming into the Discoveries Monument and Torre de Belém. It's an event that appeals to both adults and children and has captured the interest of both locals and tourists. Hippotrip is actually a fantastic concept for a family outing.

5. JAMOR ADVENTURE PARK

This thrilling adventure park is intended to get kids off their feet and up in the trees for a fun-filled trip along the Canopy. It is located 15 minutes west of Lisbon (and close to the Cruz Quebrada railway station). Participants proceed from tree to tree safely tethered and always in the company of fully qualified instructors during what is essentially an obstacle course of hanging bridges, ropes, nets, tunnels, and zip lines. Three circuits are available to be explored: the "Little Forest, geared toward children aged six to twelve; the Mega Circuit, for teenagers; and the Family Momenets, a perfect challenge for groups and families that includes 25 heart-pounding obstacles perched around 12 meters above the ground.

6. BORK KAYAK TOURS

If your kids are the daring sort, they undoubtedly think participating in some watersports would make for a fun day out. At Bork, kids can embark on a variety of sea-going sightseeing excursions organized by one of Lisbon's top nautical, subaquatic, and nature tourism companies in kayaks or on stand-up paddleboards. Children can develop their paddling abilities while exploring the Lisbon shoreline and other nearby areas, like as the stunning Arrabida coastline south of the Portuguese capital, under the instruction of an experienced adult. Surf and surf ski lessons are also offered by Bork. Dad and mom are also welcome, making an outing a special family day out. While you're on dry land, you can go on hiking and biking excursions with the help of Bork.

7. QUINTA DA REGALEIRA

Quinta da Regaleira is one of the most unexpected and peculiar tourist sites in Sintra. It is a genuine paradise of caves, grottos, and underground passageways situated inside a vast garden designed in the image of the cosmos. Its given name alludes to the Carvalho Monteiro family's vacation home, a mansion-palace opulently embellished with turrets, towers, and panoramic terraces. The building, which dates from the late 19th century, is a remarkable example of Portuguese neo-manuline architecture, and its interior is intriguing to explore.

But if you're traveling with children, the surroundings will captivate their curious brains and let their imaginations run wild. Let children explore the lakes and waterfalls, play hide-and-seek, and then follow the castellated walls that surround the estate. At one of the café tables overlooking the main house afterward, relive the adventure while sipping refreshments.

8. HILLS TRAMCAR TOUR

A tour of the city aboard a tram is a must-do activity while in Lisbon. Although the Hills Tramcar excursion is the greatest choice if you're traveling with children. The trams leave from Praca do Comercio and can be clearly identified by their retro-style red paint job. They travel on a circuit that passes through the Alfama, Graca, and Chiado neighborhoods as they traverse the city's west as far as Estrela before turning around. The history of each neighborhood and its prominent historic landmarks is explained with an audio guide. The 24-hour pass also grants free access to the Santa Justa lift, the Bica, Gloria, and Lavra funiculars, as well as the yellow public Carris trams, which include the renowned No 28 in their fleet

9. FRAGATA D. FERNANDO II E GLORIA

The wooden-hulled frigate D. Fernando II e Glória is among the best instances of antique ship preservation. It is one of the less well-known tourist attractions in Lisbon, most likely as a result of its position in Cacilhas on the opposite bank of the river Tagus. The ship is totally repaired and is kept in a dry dock, just as it was when it was first launched in 1843. This is a terrific way to keep kids occupied with a tour that provides an interesting look at life on a 19th-century battleship and has multiple decks to explore. Once on board, guests are free to explore the different levels where lifelike mannequins positioned in realistic locations assist recreate the sense of being on an ocean liner.

The eighth-oldest warship in the world is located not far from the ferry station, and visiting it is made easier by the quick and affordable river crossing from Lisbon's Cais do Sodre terminal.

10. TELECABINE LISBOA

The Parque das Nacoes telecabine, or cable car, runs above the river's edge and offers visitors a breathtaking view over the entire Nation's Park region as well as the large estuary. It takes about 20 minutes to complete the flight as the cabins float leisurely between two stations located at either end of the park (the return ticket option saves you money and offers up a different there-and-back perspective). The Altice Arena, the Oceanarium, and the impressive Vasco da Gama tower are all visible from above as you travel. Every cabin can easily fit a family, and the experience gives any visit to this area of the city a lofty dimension. The ride is a great adventure, especially for children, and the 360-degree views give a suitable wow factor to a day spent by the river.

CHAPTER SEVEN
Things you need to know before going to Portugal

Tipping is not a Portuguese norm, hence there are no hard and fast rules. It is normal to round up the bill to the closest euro or, in the case of large amounts, the nearest note in a café, restaurant, or taxi.

In Portugal, the concept of opening hours for stores, cafés, restaurants, and museums is variable. If the weather is terrible or there aren't many people around, many businesses will open late or close early (or not at all).

Transport services are drastically reduced on national public holidays.

LGBT tourists - despite its conservative history, Portugal has been more accepting of homosexuality in recent years. By default, gays have the same rights as heterosexuals because homosexuality is not mentioned in the legislation.

visa requirements

Portugal is a member of the Schengen Area, a group of 26 European nations that enables free movement of persons. As a result, nationals of any of these countries are not need to obtain a visa in order to visit Portugal for any period of time.

Meanwhile, citizens of the United Kingdom, Ireland, Canada, New Zealand, Australia, the United States, Singapore, several European non-Schengen nations, and a handful of South American countries can stay in Portugal without a visa for up to 90 days in any six-month period. Travelers must leave the

Schengen area for at least 90 days after staying 90 days before reentering. A visa is required for stays of more than 90 days.

Other nations' citizens, such as India, Pakistan, Nepal, and South Africa, will require a visa to visit Portugal. The most frequent tourist visa is a Schengen visa, which permits tourists to travel freely within the Schengen area, including Portugal, for the duration of the visa, which is normally 90 days. On the website of the Portuguese Ministry of Foreign Affairs, you can find a complete list of countries whose citizens require visas to visit Portugal.

If necessary, apply for a Schengen visa at the Portuguese embassy or consulate in your home country. If you intend to visit more than one Schengen country in addition to Portugal, apply at the embassy or consulate of the Schengen country where you intend to spend the majority of your time. Adults pay €80 and children pay €40 for a Schengen visa (aged 6-12; there is no charge for children under 6).

After arriving in Portugal, contact the Serviço de Estrangeiros e Fronteiras (Foreigners and Borders Service), which has branches in major cities, to renew a visa or a 90-day term of visa-free stay.

Citizens of Argentina, Australia, Canada, Chile, Japan, New Zealand, South Korea, and the United States can apply for holiday work visas. This type of visa permits citizens to visit Portugal for up to a year for tourism purposes and allows them to work part-time to supplement their income while in the country. This visa requires that the applicant be between the ages of 18 and 30 (31 in Peru and Australia; 35 in Canada) and that they work for no more than six months throughout their trip. This visa cannot be renewed and is only valid for one individual.

Travel tips for Portugal

The euro (€) is Portugal's currency, and notes in denominations of 5, 10, 20, 50, 100, 200, and 500 euros are available.

Except in the tiniest communities, every town has a bank. Some shops open later in the evening in Lisbon and the major Algarve resorts, and others feature automatic currency exchange machines.

Using your bank debit card to withdraw cash from an ATM (also known as a Multibanco), which can be found in even the smallest communities, is by far the most convenient way to receive money.

The voltage on the mains is 220V, which is compatible with 240V equipment. Adaptors are available at airports, supermarkets, and hardware stores for the European two round pin plug.

Cost and Money Saving Tips for Portugal

If you're wondering how much it costs to travel in Portugal, there's good news: it's still one of the most affordable locations in the EU. The costliest places to visit are undoubtedly Lisbon, Porto, and the Algarve, although even here you can get a better price on most products than in many other European countries.

In terms of how much you should budget for a trip to Portugal, if you share a room in a less costly hotel, take public transportation, and eat at low-cost restaurants, you may have a good time for between €50 and €80 per day. Staying and eating in better restaurants in the major cities will set you back more than €120 per day (albeit this won't cover your room in five-star beach resorts).

What you should avoid in Portugal?

If you don't want to attend crowded pubs and restaurants, avoid the main Algarve resort areas in the summer. Traveling in the spring or early autumn helps you to enjoy the surroundings more while also saving money.

Don't be fooled by eateries on important streets that offer tourist menus; they're always pricey, and there's a reason why locals avoid them.

While Portugal is generally secure, you should exercise caution at night in certain areas of Lisbon (such as Cais do Sodré, the top end of Avenida da Liberdade, the metro, and the Cais do Sodré–Cascais train line). Take particular caution in the darker lanes along the river in Porto.

10 Ways to Travel to Portugal on a Tight Budget

Monument to the Discoveries in Belem

It is no secret that Portugal is one of the more financially-friendly regions of Western Europe. Now, if you possess the correct knowledge, you can create amazing memories in Portugal while staying well within your budget. Here is my top 10 ways to travel to Portugal on a tight budget.

1)   Book accommodation in advance

Portugal has a multitude of affordable accommodations. But, the best way to source the cheapest deals is to book well in advance. For example, if you're traveling in August, book your accommodation in February/March.

2) Arrange transport

Travelling around Portugal can take a while. So, either take advantage of cheap public transport or hire a cheap rental car Or, you can always walk if appropriate!

3) Choose a cheaper month

Summer months are apparently the most expensive time to travel. So, maybe go in spring or early autumn. Those moments are less busy, a lot cheaper and still sunny, so you'll always be able to have a marvelous holiday.

4) Affordable flights with TAP Air

The national airline or Portugal, Tap Air, is where you can find cost-efficient deals if you book in advance. Fares are often very affordable and even the low-cost airlines will rarely beat them by much concerning price.

5) Low-cost flights to Porto

Porto is quickly becoming a brilliant destination because of its beaches, day trips and enjoyable sights. Also, a variety of low-cost airlines fly into Porto airport all the time, so take advantage of that.

6) Superb value hotels in Lisbon

Lisbon has terrific beaches and a lively nightlife, which is why so many people flock to the region. Now, you'll find a wealth of competitively priced hotels here year-round.

7)   Large resorts can fall within your budget in the Algarve

The Algarve is known for being the most expensive. But, outside of the summer months, you'll find exceptional deals at some of the larger resorts which will allow you to stay within budget.

8)   Use cafés for lunch

Cafés in Portugal usually service delicious lunches as well as tea, coffee, water etc. So, instead of heading to more expensive restaurants, enjoy a meal at a café.

9)   Use food courts for dinner

Usually you'll find the most affordable food where all the locals eat. After all, they don't want to be paying over the odds either. So, go to a local food court or shopping center and you'll find some affordable, tasty food.

10) Ask for water wherever you go

Most places in Portugal will fill up a water bottle or give you a glass of water for free. Especially places like cafés. So, instead of spending money on drinks all the time, just rely on good old-fashioned water!

14 Top Travel Tips For Portugal That'll Help You Plan A Better & A More Hassle-Free Trip

1. Travel out of peak season

Though June till September is the best time to visit Portugal, but the beautiful beaches and tourist attraction spots are usually overcrowded during this time of the year, so the best thing to do would be to visit Portugal during the shoulder season like autumn when the beaches are generally less crowded during these times and so you can enjoy a ⊡uiet time at the beaches and unwind yourself at peace.

2. Keep important documents

Before travelling to Portugal make sure that your passport is up to date and you might need at least six months if you are visiting from any part out of EU. Also by Portuguese law, you always have to carry a photo ID like driver's license with you while on your trip to Portugal.

If you are a resident of EU then you are required to bring your European Health Insurance Card.

3. Be cautious at the beach

Towns in Portugal like Ericeira, Peniche and Nazare re famous surf destinations and that is not for nothing. The beaches in these locations are popular for producing gigantic waves and some of them could be detrimentally large so much that they can even knock adults over. So while on these beaches practice precaution and keep an eye on your kids and not let them go very near the water edge.

4. Travel light to Lisbon

While traveling to the beautiful capital city of Lisbon, Portugal travel tips to remember would be to wear comfy footwear. Now, this might seem a bit absurd but especially if you are visiting the beautiful hilly city of Lisbon, the streets are cobblestone lined which might create an unstable footing and also makes the roads quite slippery. Also you need to carry on most of your outings on foot so be sure the most comfortable pair your shoes.

Another pro tip for traveling to a major destination like Lisbon, pack light. Carrying around a cumbersome luggage with you can be ⧄uite tiring. You can find pretty much anything you need in Lisbon, so the good idea is to carry only a travel backpack with the bare essentials.

5. Vegetarians – beware of the soups

Vegetarian options in Portugal restaurants are actually quite limited. You have to be prepared to eat a lot of salads. A very famous soup that you'll find in many restaurant menu is 'Coldo Verde' a very famous, tasty and traditional dish in the country. Although the soup is considered vegetarian and the waiters will also tell you the same but mostly there are a few chunks of sausage in the soup.

6. Use sun protection

If you are visiting Portugal, you are definitely going to visit the beaches. Whether you are strolling around the sand or laying on the beach or simply wandering around the cities, don't forget to use a sun block, especially between 12 P.M to 3 P.M. This is the hottest time of the day and you need to protect yourself from the heated rays of the sun.

7. Brush up your Portuguese

Odiare	Odiar	Abhorrec
Avere	Aver	Aver
Guarire	Sanar	Sanar
Udire	Oyr	Ouvir
Sperare	Esperar	Esperar
Fa caldo	Haze calor	Esta quer
Aver fame	Tener hambre	Ter Fome
Far male	Hazer mal	Fazer ma
Imitare	Ymitar	Imitar
Aumentare	Aumentar	Augment
Inabitare	Habitar	Morar
Ereditare	Heredar	Heredar
Inventare	Ynventar	Inventar
Invitare	Combidar	Convidar
Giungere	Juntar	Ajuntar
Giudicare	Juzgar	Julgar
Saltare	Saltar	Saltar
Dar de calci	Acocear	Acoucear
Amazzare	Matar	Matar
Bacciare	Besar	Beijar
Conoscere	Conocer	Conhecer
Sapere	Saber	Saber
Languire	Languir	Estardele
Ridere	Reyr	Rir

Although English is widely used in many regions of Portugal including Lisbon, Algarve and Porto, but it is not possible that every person that you come across in Portugal is versed in English and as you go outside from these major zones, you'll fewer people speaking English. So, it is recommended that before you go travelling around Portugal, brush up on your Portuguese speaking skills.

8. Check travel time duration between locations

If you are planning to visit more than one location it is necessary to check the travel time and distance between the locations that you visit. It doesn't make sense to spend your entire holiday rushing between destinations due to improper knowledge of travel itinerary.

9. Portugal Money

Money matters in Portugal and it is a great destination for budget travelling. There are ATMs in all the international airports in Portugal that that you can directly withdraw euros from. Credit cards are accepted in majority part of the country but the smaller outlets prefer taking cash only. Also keep note of the fact that every purchase that you make from your debit card will be charged, so it is necessary that you keep a tab on your expenses.

10. Safety

Although Portugal is one of the safest place around the globe, but it doesn't harm to take some precautions and know where to ask for help. If you are in need of any emergency medical service or contact the police, dial 211. It is Portugal's equivalent of 911 and this number is also toll free and does not incur any charges.

11.Make use of your G.P.S

Portugal is hands down a beautiful location to explore. But also you need to be prepared for getting lost in the midst of nowhere, especially people travelling from abroad countries, who are not used to driving on European roads and can easily be confused by the road signs and signals. G.P.S comes in handy in such situations as you can weave out of nowhere and find the road to your destination again.

12. Choose transportation wisely

If you are on budget travelling, you have to make wise decisions while choosing the mode of transport for your travelling. While car rentals and other such transportation modes can be ⊠uite costly, you can opt for travelling via the rail routes that are relatively cheaper and save a lot of your money.

13. Dine like the locals

Portuguese cuisine is generally of very supreme quality and high value so you can without any doubt stick to and anything that is grown or made locally. Also the fish and seafood in Portugal are fresh and very fine. Not to mention the equally excellent local wine. So while in Portugal you can rely on the local Portuguese food and drinks to enjoy a good meal.

14. Plan at the best time

Although you can visit Portugal all throughout the year as per your preference but if you want to enjoy a lot of outdoor fun and hanging around the beaches then you should avoid visiting Portugal during the winter months. The best time to visit Portugal would be in the summer months between June to September when weather is warm and the ocean temperature is also relatively warm, so that you can enjoy your visit to Portugal to the fullest.

CHAPTER EIGHT
Conclusion

Portugal is a terrific choice for your next vacation due to its mild weather, beautiful coastline, and fascinating cities. Everything is organized for you on an escorted vacation, from carefully picked lodging to guided tours of the best towns and landmarks.

In the cities of Lisbon and Porto, you may admire magnificent architecture, eat delectable Portuguese food, and try local port wine. Explore the Douro region's natural splendor or Madeira's subtropical vegetation on the island of Madeira. On an escorted tour, you can even visit the volcanic Azores.

Traveling in Portugal on a low budget is achievable, at least outside of the high season and when avoiding the most popular tourist attractions. Automobile rentals are inexpensive (compare prices and attempt to locate the best offers; a very cheap car may be found through Auto Europe), and gasoline is also inexpensive. Eating out is always more expensive than cooking, so rent rooms with access to a kitchen if you want to save money. You might also look into cost-free lodging choices like couch-surfing and house-sitting, especially if you plan to stay in the nation for a longer period of time than just a holiday.

Printed in Great Britain
by Amazon